Descended from salt water.

A *poetry collection*
S. M. L. YAU

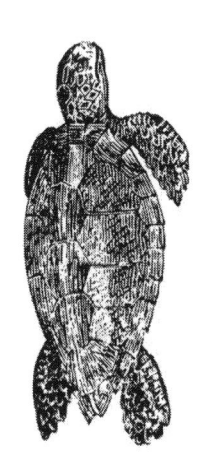

Copyright © 2021 by Samantha Yau

Cover Design via Canva

All internal illustrations by Serina Yasmin (*@ssycreates*, Instagram)

All rights reserved.

This book or any portion thereof may not be reproduced or used in any manner whatsoever without the express written permission of the publisher except for the use of brief quotations in a book review.

I dedicate this to my loved ones, passed on and here still.

For my sisters, Sadé and Sophia.

For my life, Ca'olin.

For my friends, Sabrina and Serina.

"You think your pain and your heartbreak are unprecedented in the history of the world, but then you read."

James Baldwin.

I am often asked,

Why does your father have an English name?

Isn't he from China?

Isn't he Chinese?

If only you knew the ignorance stemming from your thoughts, branching out of your mouth and dripping down into your words. If only you knew the pain that strikes from those.

China, a country I've never seen. Never been.

It is the birthing country, a motherland.

But you are Chinese? Yes and no.

I am a daughter of Hong Kong. The harbour of incense. Island children found to the south. Where we speak in Cantonese and drink milk tea. Shaped by being an old colony, traded under duress. By your country. By my country. The one I own a piece of. The one I was born in.

My father has an English name because it made life easier. For foreign tongues not to twist and choke. For foreign tongues to not learn their place. To accommodate.

- What's in a name?, *shortlisted in the Folklore Prize 2020.*

It's been heavy on my mind,

Drowning the time I have spare,
Do you ever think of me?
Do you ever seem to find,
That you harbour a place laid bare,
For the notion of the 'us' you see?
The load gets lighter with the passing of time,
The idea that you loved me or once did care,
Now could you listen to this last plea?
Because it's been heavy on my mind,
Drowning the time I have spare,
Do you ever think of me?

- Anymore.

Where were you?
When I needed you.
How were you?
When I needed you.
What were you?
When I needed you.
Why were you,
all the reasons
contained in my tears?
I'll never know why but I
always knew.
That I had been given a
world, half-decayed.

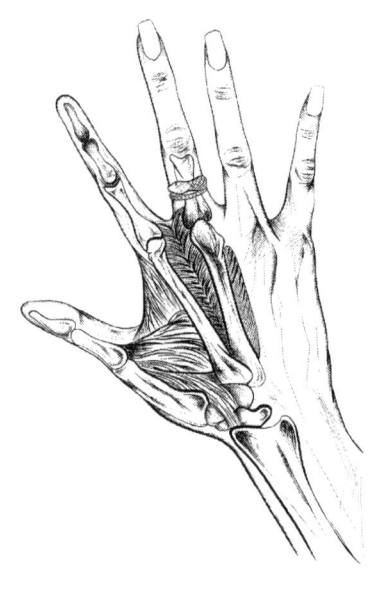

- The bones left behind.

My grandfather showed me his `hatred`
for the dusting of night in his skin.
And in return, I learnt to acknowledge mine without it.

- Undoing.

Father,

who was once good,
who grew bitter over lost love,
who chose to strike out with absence,
who remained absent,
who became a father again.
Did you want to forget us,
Father?

- Something I learnt at five years old.

A tower of strength
languidly looming
carefully choosing
The battles stood for
The battles to lose
Yet far below the walls
The foundations below were
crumbling critically
disaster doomed
Betrayed by selflessness
And as day turned to night
And regret rapidly rose
It could no longer continue to be
The tower of strength that
They needed it to be
Slender shoulders no longer able
to bear the brunt of the burden.

- Innocence.

In the East / I am west / In the West / I am east / *Unacceptable / Undesirable /* somewhere in between

- Halves of a whole.

The screams of my sister still true in my ears / this is not my home / the wailing of the ancestors to not forget / the want to be like them and not like me / to wish away my eyes that edged toward heaven / that were dark rounds in a round face / skin that was coffee and cream my mother said / I did not like coffee / I wanted to go back to what I knew / but now I had been here so long that I forgot how to conjure the language that stirred in my forebears mouths / I buried it deep in gunpowder shame / my tongues chewed and swallowed / rotated from red rouge and cream flowers into white skies and crimson crosses / an anomaly in all the places I drew breath / my mouth a smoking barrel

- The loss in the soil.

Am I someone you won't talk about?

What if my name, wraps around your tongue,
Blisters your lips into vermilion?
What if this wound never closes for you,
What if the memory of me grows without grace?
But in the dark.

- The rose.

I see the others,

who inherited their mother's eyes.

Their mother's sweetness. Their mother's dimples. Their father's expressions.

Their father's laughter. Their father's pride.

I wonder why this is so, the reasoning and the chances of what it is we receive.

What were the chances?

As I see myself,

who inherited my mother's resent.

My mother's pain. My mother's bitterness. My father's spite. My father's hatred.

My father's absence.

I wonder why this is so, when I see the others.

- Heirlooms.

The boy at school who has never spoken to me, asks me why I have an Asian last name.

Because I am Asian.

But, ain't your Mom married? (*She must be a Thai bride, or a whore*)

Was.

So, why don't you have your Dad's name? (*She must be a whore*)

I do.

But how?

Because my father is Chinese.

Oh, your Mom is the white one not your Dad? *(That don't happen!)*

She is mostly white, I guess.

I bet your Dad is rich. (*It wasn't for anything else*)

Once, I wouldn't know.

Huh, why not?

He chose not to be in my life.

But Chinese people take care of their family don't they? (*That can't be true*)

Probably?

I thought you were posh and clever. (*This is no longer amusing*)

I'm a council estate kid from Acocks Green, I grew up in dirt with drugs and criminals and thieves and hunger and

neglect and no I do not speak Chinese and no, I am not good at Maths and no, I do not have a 'tiger' Mom, she is far more invested in men and their money.
And suddenly, I am Chinese enough, but not.
The boy goes quiet.

- Not an educated, red brick, hard working, number whizz, *after Sean Wai Keung's 'you are mistaken'.*

He looked to the stars and found my true name just one.
This was a knowing that would pave my being,
one that became me and this gives me peace.

- Gung gung/公公.

Young love,

with the amber skin,

with the shapely eyes,

with the sable hair,

Young love,

with the wide nose,

with the full lips,

with the freckles there,

Young love,

with the sadness sunken in,

with the eyes that look down,

with the love forgotten now,

Young love,

you're breaking my heart.

- At six, I prayed to God to make me white.

Mother,

who raised you with their pain,
who caused you to hurt,
who taught you lessons the hard way,
they needed more time to become your Mother.

- Things I learnt at twelve.

Kai je sends my grandmother steaks wrapped in frozen paper every fourth Sunday. She is grateful, yet, doesn't understand why he does this kindness. His house in Bristol is full of laughter and cousins who look just like me. He runs a little take away along the shore of Burnham-on-Sea and it is his pride and joy. I beg to go. Kai je speaks to me in Cantonese, I nod and he smiles.

- Mr Lin.

A woman can birth a child.

An agony.
A grief.
A *reminder*.

- Bitterness.

Both of my parents were born in July and it was a month swimming in sunshine, this was where the fun began this time as my aunties brought us to a little farm, somewhere between Solihull and Henley. Golden rays drowned us in warmth and we children knew what we would be asked to do. Silken strawberries are the rubies we mined for that day, find the largest or the most odd and the victory spoils were all yours. Their lustrous drippings sat sticky sweet upon my chin along with the soil buried under my nails. The punnet was brimming with creamy pink flesh and green hats tipping. That summer morning lasted until night and I wished for just one more sweet bite.

- Strawberry Picking, *after Seamus Heaney's 'Blackberry Picking' and Robert Frost's 'After Apple-Picking'.*

There is an ocean behind my eyes

that is waiting to forgive.
And yet, it begs, begs to be released.
But I, swallow it down, until I am afloat.
But I, would rather drown, until I choke.
But I, stutter and look away, until I am engrossed,
and I betray, the one thing that loves me most.

- But it won't.

Her eyes sank into mine.

She looked upon me as if
I might turn to dust.
Scattered across the dirt with lost
letters and names now forgotten.
With a name not truly her own, but
a shield.
You child, are heard by God.
It is who you are, the name you hold,
that you will carry through this life,
wear it with pride, do it justice.

- Grandmother's lost language, *after Ocean Vuong*'s '*Kissing in Vietnamese*'.

Taiwan.

Whose blood ran thick for centuries upon cold streets.

Hong Kong.

Whose freedom trickles down through the knuckles of oppression.

You are loved.

Unforgotten.

- Heritage.

A man stands at the doors of the supermarket and he is the first in line to enter. He huffs. He lets his eyes wander around and pauses when he meets mine.

But there is something stirring, something brewing upon his face, now contorted. Hideous. The mask covering his nose and mouth, hides a frown of disgust. That I exist.

The doors drag along their tracks to open, a wave of relief with it. I sigh. I am now first in line.

- 2020.

My grandmother would sit and watch birds with me for hours from her little patio / not a word whispered but conversations afloat above the tiled roof in our bustling suburb / the place / my haven / and both of us would sit in glee / at the many visitors we would have / making notes of jackdaw / chaffinch / and little red robins / who she claimed were her lost loved ones watching over us / my grandmother had soft eyes / hidden behind a wit-filled tongue that cut like a knife and thick skin / she walked life alone / and yet spent her time devoted to creatures so small / she knew I wished for wings too

- How my grandmother taught me to hope.

Eat every grain, every last one.

The ancestors harvested them,

From sunrise to sunset,

dusk to dawn.

Below,

inside my bowl,

the humble grain sits.

And I hear my ancestors weep and call for

The pains in their backs, the sun on their face,

The pearls of sweat that rolled

down their necks,

Below, inside their own bowls,

the humble grain sat.

They are in every grain, every last one.

- Mai faan.

Say these words and you may eat.

Drink these words and your children may eat.

Change your name, your being and you will be forgiven.

Forgiven for seeking refuge in the darkest hour,

forgiven for your savagery, the language and harmonies trapped inside your words.

Forgiven for the melanin that darkens in the sun.

This is no church
of
mine.

- Missionary.

That familiar pang
of insides hardened
The lull of the wave
does not bring sleep

Children try to hang
on her tired legs
Yet still she is tall
and does not weep

To water she sprang
safer than eyes forced
closed by poverty
survival's reap

Hopeful songs that rang
chimed inside her ears
A new beginning
dawns in the deep

- After the Hunger & before Typhoon Mary.

Elegant hands stretch
out further this time,
it is a warm Autumn day and
the leaves have fallen,
from the surface it appears
that nothing remarkable is happening,
under the ground and inside of the dirt
something *is* happening,
muddied and wet and warm
soaked in earth and the rot of
other things,
my fingers are a flurry of branches
that stir in the brisk wind.

- Some work is quiet.

Grandmother's bedroom is coated in specks of God between solemn pages.

Books line the walls as ivy in a country garden and there is creation in her voice as she recalls her reveries.

Unbreaking.

Stories of blacksmiths upon the maypole, of her father tilting his hat to every passerby, to her mother saving sweet rations for her own indulgence.

How she was not permitted to be.

Instead, to work. Expected to marry.

Psalm 23 sits open upon her pillow and she is the shepherd of dreams.

- Una.

Yᴏᴜ fed your children to the wolves.

- Gone.

Almond eyes from afar.

Raven hair, glossy and dark.
A face belonging to her father.
An unfortunate indicator that glared in the reflection of the glass.
That stabbed at her mother's words.

- The reminding, *after Warsan Shire's 'Your Mother's First Kiss'.*

I wish I could be as soft and serene as the waves
> that brush the beach sand.

Instead, I am a *force*
> to be reckoned with,

a torrent,
> the daughter of a typhoon.

- Unapologetic.

That night	**T**hat morning
The fire devoured its way	The smoke slithered
into our home	into our home
Through the front door,	Through the front door,
spilling through the oil	sinking through the oil
Drowning	Drowned
My mother	My mother
and her children.	Into a shadow who did
What was a family died	choose evil ~~love~~
instead.	instead.
My sisters, a shell.	A woman, a hollow.
My sisters, a shell.	A woman, a hollow.
I try to wash it from my	She tries to sink it
skin, scrub until	into her skin, swims until
I am flakes of debris.	she is a part of him.
There is no reprieve to	There is now reprieve to
be had.	be had.
Bare foot, I run.	Her feet, concreted.
I don't know where.	She doesn't care where.
I am not coming back.	There is no going back.

- The path, *after Tay Reem's 'I Have a Secret'.*

Gratitude, this word so heavy

sits atop and at the forefront of
the paper thoughts, that stack themselves
up so high, out of reach and
out of sight
Gratitude, runs parallel to the misery
underneath the tight rope that
I balance along, tension triggers the traces of
hesitation and I am no longer
walking but running
from the cognation
an evasion of this life that I feel
desperation to escape
Gratitude, there is no beauty to be found
in the pain I lay down here
for I am peeling back the fine layers of skin
until there is nothing but
raw flesh wilting around my feet
Gratitude, slips away and as do I
as do I.

- Grey cuttings.

You keep pouring your love away into empty vessels. Don't you realise that it is pure gold?

- Gratitude.

It is 1841 and there is a crisis running through the veins and guts of the people, a disease that came upon ships and along roads. Poppies flourish. A mother weeps.

It is 1843 and there is a crisis running through a barren, forgotten land. The weight of the Crown upon the island, it sinks and it sinks and it sinks under the word 'perpetuity'.

It is 1941 and there is a crisis running through the world. Its name is Tyranny. Tyranny knows no boundaries. It is the crimson that ribbons out, seeps into the soil and between legs. A woman weeps.

It is 1945 and there is an opportunity running from the past and toward the future.

It is 1997 and there is static thunder suffocating, running through the air. My father is thirty seven this day and inhales sharply. Freedom's shadow pales in the wake of a new morning, deliverance swelling in constraint's tight fist.

It is 2014 and there is a crisis running through the generations. A sea of citrus yellow, occupies, floods its streets. Umbrellas not only protect from the rain it seems.

It is 2020 and there is a crisis running through the islands. Where mouths are sewn shut with silk fear. Hong Kong weeps.

- The land is alive, *after Nikita Gill*'s '*Partition*'.

She spoke only in the tongue of her mother.

Hakka.

A losing language.

Losing to the mellow melody of Mandarin.

Losing to the candid courage of Cantonese.

Hers was earthy, rough and raw.

Modest and humble.

Without flaw.

- Po Po/婆婆.

A child of two cities,
A child between two worlds,
A child of the mountains and the sea,
Trapped in the land locked city that gave me a home.

- Unbelonging.

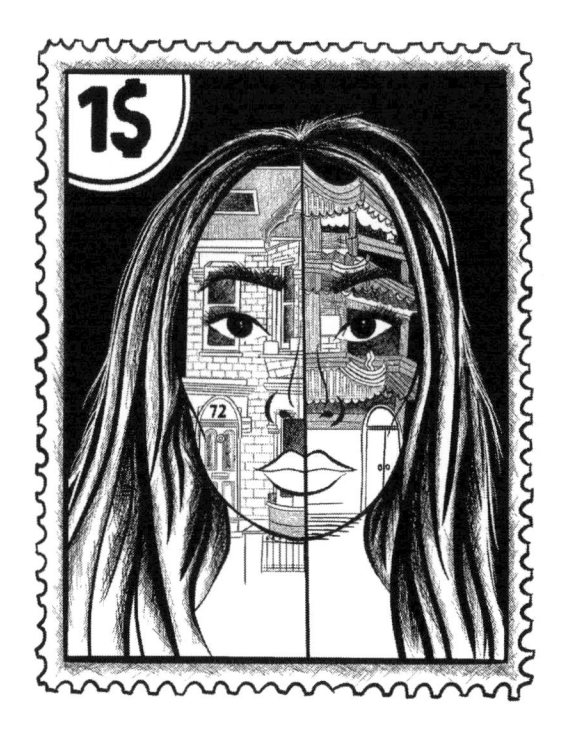

Mother breaks apart the chicken / bare hands on bare skin / rummages through its bones and flesh with ease and care / yet without thought / its wetness swims in soy sauce and fresh ginger and fresh garlic / she adds a pinch of sugar / it sits in the brine / its pink middle turning to a dark brown / its skin once dull now glossy / she says she will teach me how when I have hands big enough to hold a knife and a mouth big enough to maim / to do the same with my own daughters

- Preparation, *after Jihyun Yun's 'All Female'*.

He sits with me in the calm of morning, walks alongside me in the quiet of a lonely wood stroll, is the guilt that stifles my laughter. He is the reminder I once loved. Grief is an old friend.

- Bittersweet.

I would have burnt out every light to have you love me,
I would have turned the sea tides and drowned lands,
I would have set fire to the forests and uprooted it all,
I would have pulled the plug on all the lakes and watched life wither,
I would have taken the moon from its orbit without hesitation.

Just to know what it felt like for an *instance*.

- Abandoned.

I was swimming in my own body.

My own body of water.

Lakes for lungs. Overwhelming tides.

Drowning. Gasping for air that would not be gasped.

Fighting for space that would not be made.

Searching for the shallows to wade.

I remember waking that day.

Salt sat in the depressions of my skin.

Crystals of it upon my lips.

I was many shades of blue that month.

- The one who knocks.

Mother, please. When those men come knocking. And they do, they always do. Do not let them in, for their smiles are false. Your lovers were all vultures circling for a feast. They brace for a meal that they know they will not thank you for. You, with your broken heart, your pity, your wallowing. You will not find homes in their bodies, they will not come home to yours. They are not here to love, but to peel back your flesh and to wear it and to pick at the carcass you supply so willingly. And you, you have forgotten your children before. Little legs and little eyes and little hands who wanted you to be happy but not at the cost of innocence. We grew tired of you eating their words. At their greedy stares as we grew from girls to women.

- The vultures, *after Yrsa Daley-Ward's 'mum'*.

Anguish began when the boys thought they were men and when my body thought me a woman. I was no longer just flesh and bones, but flesh and bones they thought
An experience,
    a tour,
        a collectable,
           a souvenir,
              a colony.
When they asked if I was different in taste, when they placed their hands where they didn't belong, when they asked if I was firmer, tighter, when they told me to smile. I instead bared my teeth, on instinct, because I have known this greed, along with all the women inside of me.

- Men.

Ceaseless memories,

Will you end? Do you end?
For I haven't
the time,
to tumultuously turn,
thoughts through this thinker.
I tell myself that these will end,
As night ends and dawn begins,
As winter crashes and spring rises,
As rivers begin and seas swallow lines along the shore.
Ceaseless memories, seemingly stay.
As night returns and day is hidden,
As winter promises and spring fades,
As rivers end and seas perish.

- Cycles.

Your face drifts

through the rooms
from the photos that sit
silently
inside the draw
waiting in the minutes
hours
and the days
to be found again.
In the dust collected upon
a sock from a pair
the glasses from a case
how you have settled
in everything I ever loved.

- It comes in waves.

T hinking, overthinking, analysing, observing, assuming, surmising, presumptions. All of these things, horrid things.
They hurt you more than you know.

- Stop.

White noise, grey scale, slow motion, on mute.
This is what it felt *like*.
Nothingness is absence.
A murder of crows, sat perched.
Dark clouds surrounding, cut from the sky
and into the mind.
An end, oh to end would be just fine,
for the crows have murder on their minds.

- The melancholy.

The man at the stall points with his worn cleaver / hands sodden and his forehead browned from long days / brown flesh is seated on the wood / she is the most delicate he says / and he draws my eyes to her striking skeleton / I pause for too long / the man points again / I nod and smile as I have been taught / you daydream too much child / hurried steps on the ferry home are heavy with wishes to be swimming instead / the kitchen is fragrant / we watch mother cast her parts away / the parts she said were not sweet enough / father ravages the white and the brown and the ginger and the spring onion / I swallow every last ounce / hoping she will make me sweeter

- Pickings.

I am

deep rooted,

intertwined,

laced together,

woven heavily,

with the trammels of my past.

And they wonder why I am difficult to love.

I am the sand within the mangroves.

- Bare.

They only spoke Hakka,
very loud and very fast.
I could not answer them-
I could not understand them.

They wore dark linen,
and calloused hands,
weathered and worn and weary,
strong and smooth and sore,
Carrying the faces that,
carried my nostalgia.

They farmed lands,
as brown as,
their driftwood skin,
cast out,
root and stem,
surviving anew.

Atop the hills,
where the sun bore down,
upon their wide brimmed hats,
and houses of round,
they blossomed,
despite the droughts.

A final glimpse,
I try to speak out,
I try to reach,
but they cannot hear,
my pleading,
over their songs.

They only spoke Hakka,
very loud and very fast.
I could not answer them-
I could not understand them.

- Dandelion women, *after Norman MacCaig's 'Aunt Julia'.*

Words that cut are difficult to hold yet difficult to let go.
They cling to the air, I try to contain for too long in my chest.
They feel heavier, in the water I try to hold up in my palms.
They seep into my skin and they are the flames that force sweat to trickle along the dimples in my back.
Words that cut, cut deeper still,
they have set me free.
From you.

- Set loose.

Are you honest, are you gentle?
For I have been broken
and put back together
I have been built up
and torn down, stripped of
trust and given the expectation that
everything leaves agony
everything leaves.

- Scarring.

A baptism of fire, the one you ignited and left behind
in me,
thank you.
I am reborn like a forest from a
flame.

- Reemergence.

Dear ancestors,

As I write this, I think of you. I try to picture your faces. I try to picture the fine lines drawn across your tanned, leathery skin, like rivers strewn across a map. I try to imagine the language you use, the tones and beauty of it. I try to place my hand on yours but cannot feel the warmth. I try to hear what you say, but I think I try too hard.

While I know that we are poles apart and the language between us lost, I want you to know that you are loved. Loved each time I burn the paper belongings for you to enjoy and be fond of. Each time I share lei cha, or give the eldest elder the eye of the fish, each time I smell stinky tofu, each time I feel that the new year has come, delivered from the new moon.

Watch over me and I will continue to think of you.

Yours.

- Those who came before.

The dew that sat upon the webs you wove,

As I approached, there was nothing pretty about these gossamers.

They were acrid with your lies.

They were clung to everything you had once touched, even me.

- Midas.

The sunrise stirred the shadows away,

Songbirds sang, night did stop,
So surreal in my mind's eye,
I stretched to soothe my sore aches,
I slid to the window,
Such was that day,
I swore to honour you, to be sincere,
The sunset slowly saluted the stars,
Songbirds sighed and night did start.

- The morning after we lost you.

My mother held onto the cards that were left behind
by the flowers,
paper and petals scattered across the concrete.
Tears rolled from her lilac-grey eyes and I couldn't help.
Bang. Scream.
It played out and danced in the reflections of the pools
that poured. Whisperings of a childhood that were once
haunting,
still haunting.
Her mother and father hold knives at each other's
throats, cutting each other with words and the still stares.
Her cheeks now scarlet, scarred from the salt streams.
Did she see this as the end of those, or did something stir
in the hatred and the love and the despair as she stood at
the foot of her father's casket? Her father was gone yet
still remained in her lilac-grey eyes,
the ashes of his legacy tainting her memory.

- The stories we carry.

Punctured hearts diminish dreams into the thinnest air / that throbbing there / that sits inside your fingertips of frost / Father / lingers into bruises of black / Mother / then blue / then green / then yellow / back to black / buried skin deep / such pretty scars / when all you needed to do was love / your three daughters inherited that which should have been burned / upon the pyre of our parted parents / its thick smoke choking / for there would be no money / no dowry / by having three daughters / that would stop the pain of having no sons

- 三千金, *after Mary Jean Chan's 'The Heart of the Matter'.*

The morning I found your name, ringing between my
ears, synchronised, with the lashings of salt tears
hurtling along my skin. Salt into open wounds.

This I won't forget.
Let me return to you now as I sit here again.

This morning I find your name, ringing between my ears,
synchronised, with the lashings of salt tears
hurtling along my skin. Salt onto scars.

They say time does heal, you heal in time. Time
went on with your name imprinted in my mind.

- Kristian.

The hardy grit exterior that I wear on my skin,

laden across every inch,

    it's there for a reason,

        don't doubt why.

- The mask.

A band of pale green jade / sat so prettily on my Mother's left wrist / the proud mark of a married woman / I had always admired the way her moon like skin complemented its shine / how her green veins sat basking in its beauty / how it still shone so brightly / despite the lustre of love / her eyes once held / for a man / not worthy of her light / faded / but not her prized jade bangle / still lingering near her heart

- My mother wears her heartbreak well/玉.

A mistake, once. A choice, again and again and again.

- No excuses.

August rains, how you betray

I know this sun that bears down

yellowing my skin into amber

won't last- along

with the notions

that fly as sparrows in

murmuration to hide

the weight of the words

that are so often spoken

behind closed doors

and low to floors

some words pay praise

and some charge high

some are spoken for the sake of

speaking

and I grow tired of being awake

sometimes

because some speak in flowers

and some are the poison

that breed in society's nest

and I've ignored the August sun

for a moment too long

my skin now flushed redder

than the flags I grew upon

and how remorseless that shade is

I will be gold by the end of the hour
But not the same as the
gold craved
From the pit of the earth
How they both lend so bold and
radically
To my hands and form tonight

- Gold after *Audre Lorde's 'Coal'*.

I can still remember how hollow her face was.

She had been unmothered. How that year went by, how her sister held her.

How life cruelly continued coaxing clocks to tease time to and fro.

Tanned shoulders against the blue wall he once stood up against, now grey.

Everything coated in a blanket of dust, his mother did not want to wash him away from the world, from her home, his ashen embrace.

- The pit.

Wastelands in place of oceans / all of the men I have known / grandfather / father / cousins / partner / friends / rib of my rib / whose mouth squeezes it from the air / whose blood boils until it is tar / dripping from the pores / whose tears are strangled until they evaporate from the plains / who cannot come to speak of hurt without bruises being dealt over and over and over

- Hearts of men.

Still waters run deep.

Too deep. And I've been running my whole life.

- Fear.

That winter morning

eventually turns to a

slow sigh from spring's mouth.

- A haiku, *after Sonia Sanchez's 'i count the morning'.*

Do you want to know the worst of it?

I cannot remember your face in whole.

Your voice,

your jawline,

the flecks of gold in your eyes,

your laughter.

My mind attempts in vain to conjure the freckles that perhaps

sat on the bridge of your nose. The wrinkles that creased at the edges of your eyes.

Its attempt at reconstructing what I thought was.

It was not enough.

I feel robbed in more ways than one, by loss.

- Recollection.

It feels like crossing a desert, only to welcome nothing on the other side / it is an *unfeeling* / I claim that I cannot miss what I have never known / but I drip lies like salt over pineapple flesh / I miscount the sugars in my coffee on purpose / because bitterness has taken a plunging hold / I feel betrayal on my tongue / it stabs stabs stabs with sour familiarity / to know that sweetness is alien and that you made your choice without hesitation

- The choices.

There is a bitter tone to her voice that
Is filled with the ugly and the beautiful
Her father was shot at while collecting money and
He returns each Friday and arrives through the front
door with red poison breath and red fists curled

Her father, golden and gargantuan
with coarse hair that her mother, halfway between the
English country and Calabria, combs carefully with oils
Staring at the scars she stabbed into his skin
Half this place and half another

His own father was a bloodied brute of
Liverpool and Livery Street, his own mother a beaten bag
From grammar school to this ill life
My mother's mother followed suit,
my mother's father another spoke in a wheel

Turning time through the sand at Sandy Lane
In the middle of old Sparkbrook
Where the Irish families lived with Pakistani ones,
The rank and file stuck in a rut and a pit
With the pimps and the pimped

With the drugs and the gangs standing in line, to be
working class was and is a crime
Where desperation drives you down a road in a car that
you are a mere passenger, left rotting under the hot
summer sun with dog shit dried to white

And she bleeds at the chaos you're born from
Because it's all you've ever known
it's all you've ever known.

- When My Mother Says Birmingham, *after Colin Tan's 'Let Me Bleed' and Jenny Mitchell's 'When My Mother Says Jamaica'*.

That night, the universe reminded me of the grief circling in my throat.

- The mourning.

Y̲ou came, you made your impression and you were gone within a whisper.

- Hurricane.

I remember not going to school for what felt like two months / I would count the number of lines in the paper on the wall of the hostel / But I could not count the days I had been without a home / My mother would lament for a man she had made a home in / And I wished to be elsewhere too / My sister says she does not remember any of it and I think that's her way of processing the pain of being unwanted. I believe her / I try to understand but I do not / I would not forget the number of lines in the paper on the wall of the hostel

- What remains.

It has taken me a long time to realise that my soul is weeping.

- Body of water, *after Nayyirah Waheed*'s *'yield'*.

The resolve,

that sits here in my heart,

that seeps from my every pore,

that emanates from my being,

I remember God,

I remember the prayers I whispered.

For that same resolve.

- The answers.

You and I,

One in the same, the same in one,

Our eyes saw, our voices spoke, our minds thought.

You were the calm and I was the rage.

You were the forgiving and I was the blame.

Without you, nothing would be what it is today for you and I.

- Her, for Sophia.

I am now unashamedly, both a native and immigrant child, wherever I am
and wherever
I go.

- Bound by blood.

T he man in the kitchen, stands arms crossed over his chest, as mangled branches that should have been cut back in winter and he watches me pour milk into my tea, claims this is not tea, claims I am doing it wrong, claims I should try matcha. I drench my throat in the brew and my eyes do not drop from his, I want him to watch.

He chokes.

- Cha.

Be kinder to your sisters.

Speak up to those who need it,
even if you share blood.
Never hold your tongue again.

- Things I learnt at twenty one.

There was a time when I thought you were the world,

when what you said was gospel,

hung upon every word.

And yet you, still smoke, still stung, slept silently as I prayed.

A

    False

        God.

I still consider us acquaintances you know. Your words stained the tongue of my father as he devoured gratefully, his bowl of humble rice and fish each Friday.

- The myth.

It wasn't working.

For I was hidden away in a shell. Not able to be honest. Not able to be. How could I explain myself to someone when I held back. Held my emotions, as water that rushes toward a dam. Blinking fast to push the same rushes of water. Laced with fear. Along with my words that were now braiding in the air of the room. I did not like difficult conversations. I was not taught to listen. I was forced to fight in my defence like a dog in the dirt, yelping on its belly. When I was done. He simply held me. And I could let the rain pour, and stop the drought.

- The desert was once a sea.

Before their departure, they were
praying and living along a pipe

> dream that had been smothered in hope
> like their mother's farewell kisses that

stretched for them across a lonely
land that wanted their bodies and

> their cheap labour in vast demand
> and in 39 to supply the fuel of

the lust of money and man and
the newspapers only know them as

> the 39 who grasped at lorry doors in
> search of air that did not exist for

them to survive on but only
enough to send farewell kisses that

> would not reach their mothers in time
> their voices thin at the end of a phone line

before their departure, they were people

who laughed and lived and.

- In memory of the 39 Vietnamese who died in search of hope.

Despite the suffering,

    The long winter nights,
The stubbornness of the typhoons
    and monsoon rains,
She bloomed with vitality and strength.

- Bauhinia blakeana, for Sadé.

Love is not,

Swallowing every treacle-filled word,

That is seething with control.

Love is not,

Feeling it slip down your throat,

Along with the crimson ladder from your broken nose.

Love is not,

Digesting the blows to your body,

Painted red, for them to feel whole.

- How it begins and how it takes hold.

Of all the things you hold, your spirit, the water, the home you have made, the bed where you lay. I pray that you found your happiness.

- Despite it all.

My women with

raven hair
and skin of gold
and earthen eyes
of the night sky reflected now,
not earthen at all but *heavenly*
how glorious you are

- Hooded, round, narrow, monolids.

That day she picked us up. The car still running. Terror painted across her milky face.
Dotted tears still raw, clinging to the bottom of her chin.
Dark curls fell across her steel grey eyes. Those same curls spelt
out the elephant in the room on her cheek.
Don't.
    Don't.
        Don't.
Be normal. Please.
I knew. But I knew not to.
Holes carved in the walls. Fist holes
like bullet holes laid into the plaster. She glared
and I glared in return. I could not live in the violence she wrapped up neatly in silence.

        I could not live in this prison of his.

- The burdens in our rib cages.

Fortune. I think you are mine.

Your voice wishing good morning whispers onto the nape of my neck. Your lips widening to greet happiness at the door. Your dark eyes playfully dancing with the gold in mine. Your hands holding me each time I have fallen apart (there have been many). Your hands which pulled me back together (there will be many more). The one love I can rely upon to not fail, when I do.

- Wealth.

My mother would go on
endlessly
about how she
hated
the taste of salt
All while knowing

                                                    I was
                                              descended
                                         from its water

- Descended from salt water.

The winter sun bowed itself before the skyline,

Shadows stirred and the night did arrive,

As it did, I felt no joy, I didn't welcome the coldness that came,

the midnight coloured evenings, the frost that sat on the earth at dawn.

The woe of winter wrapped itself around me

and it always let go in

its own time.

- Winter's break.

And those were the days,

when I was,

weaker,

meeker,

hushed,

crushed,

unspoken,

broken,

tormented,

discontented,

by sheer cruel contempt,

Let me make this clear.

                              Those days are long gone.

-    Here it is.

Descended from salt water. - S. M. L. Yau

Some moments linger on

for too long

Between the spaces of

hushed words

and hard pressed actions

The woman in front of me

scrolls past

The face of a man-

Hair as white as paper

Skin as pearlescent as the neon

reflections in the delta back home- that

Could have been my father

My popo

my gung gung

an elder

And she likes the photo of

A female 'self-made' millionaire

And I am waves of pain

That reflect only to myself

And I am waves of rain

That reflect only to repel

I wonder who gets out of this

Alive and not shattered

Alive and not battered

She moves along

And I am held no longer by the blood
Or the roots of a home from home or
the motherlands
But something else that runs
Deeper than the labels that
Cling to my arms
And I weep rivers this day.

- Vicha Ratanapakdee.

How do I explain to the man,

handing me the application form,

that I am not just a [tick] box of 'Asian',

but I am a migrant within a homeland,

but I am an immigrant in another,

but people running into dark water,

because the land was no longer safe,

and struggle and hunger,

and lost legacy and pain,

but I [tick] the box anyway,

and how it aches.

- Layers.

There are times
>   when you feel you are not
enough.
>   These times must be swallowed
like the sea does the shore.

- Crest of a wave.

I cried the Lunar New Year / where I watched with trepidation / your clumsy hands folding your shrimp and chive dumplings / my own wrapping vegetable ones / our little fingers / working until they were cold and wet and raw / working until our ancestors felt our plight / we were not alone in that kitchen that day / I am sure gung gung and popo were with us / as we wrapped our heritage up into little pastries / laughed in delight at our first attempts / the learning that we never received / that we were robbed of / and how delectable they were and would never be again

- In our skins.

These hands that once held me close,

These hands that caused hell to harken and halt.

These hands that promised to help.

These hands that instead hampered the one thing they were meant to heighten.

These hands that haunt my memories -

hold onto them, tenterhooks ensnared.

These hands of mine, will not harvest your crops or harden in the harrowing sun.

These hands of mine, will harness the harmonies of hope that yours tried to hang.

- Handle with care.

I think it will take all the suns
and seeds to make my soul spring
flowers *again*.

- Regeneration.

It's been a long time coming, for this truth to be
unveiled,
for it to become known.
>
> But

I am not unfortunate or accursed,

I am not regrettable.

This feeling that had become immersed,

Like a flaming crucible.

Was a lie that others had lived, a make believe.

Easier to swallow and hold,

Did it make you feel better at night's eve?

Oh how you can make sense of it all as you grow old.

- Growing older was a gift to me.

I wish I could hand you my eyes,

For you to adorn,

Over your own,

To see your image, as I do.

- No rose tints.

She is

multitudes

volumes

collections

compilations

series

of captivating softness.

- Woman of colour.

I wonder if I am Chinese enough when I use chopsticks
I wonder if I am Chinese enough with my British passport
I wonder if I am Chinese enough when I use a knife and fork
I wonder if I am Chinese enough when I eat dim sum on a Saturday lunch time
I wonder if I am Chinese enough when I eat chips and beans on a Friday night
I wonder if I am Chinese enough when they want me to speak in Cantonese though broken
I wonder if I am Chinese enough I speak in English though so well
I wonder if I am Chinese enough when I burn incense and think of them
I wonder if I am Chinese enough when I sob in Catholic cemeteries
I wonder if I am Chinese enough when the man sneers nihao on the street
I wonder if I am Chinese enough when I say thank you instead of mm goi and dor je
I wonder if I am Chinese enough when they find out I once lived in Hong Kong
I wonder if I am Chinese enough when the girl pulls her eyes up for a photo

I wonder if I am Chinese enough when they find out my father abandoned me
I wonder if I am Chinese enough when the boy touches me because he wants to try Chinese
I wonder if I am Chinese enough when I get called a chink
I wonder if I am Chinese enough when I have to ask what something means
I wonder if I am Chinese enough when I say my own name
I wonder if I am Chinese enough with my accent
I wonder if I am Chinese enough when I am born in a homeland away from a homeland away from a homeland
I wonder if I am Chinese enough when I get called a gweilo
I wonder if I am Chinese

- I am.

Descended from salt water. - S. M. L. Yau

Heavy was the wind that rushed through
your grandfather's hair that day
A cold wind that carried the
Colder embrace of a country
That wanted their labour
And labour's hard-earned fruit
But not their dark bodies
That sullied the joy of the harvest

Heavy was the wind that pushed
The boats across seas
Carried my grandparents
Away from a homeland
Where food scarce
And freedom sparse
The beautiful island and the harbour
A haven from the hunger

I did not dream that this union
was one so similar
not foreign not opposite
yet akin
Grasping for opportunity in
A wealth so common

Where do we go from here?
You and I, children of immigration
What do we lay out for the wind to push
For the children to come
From the wombs
Of us

- When worlds collide, for Ca'olin.

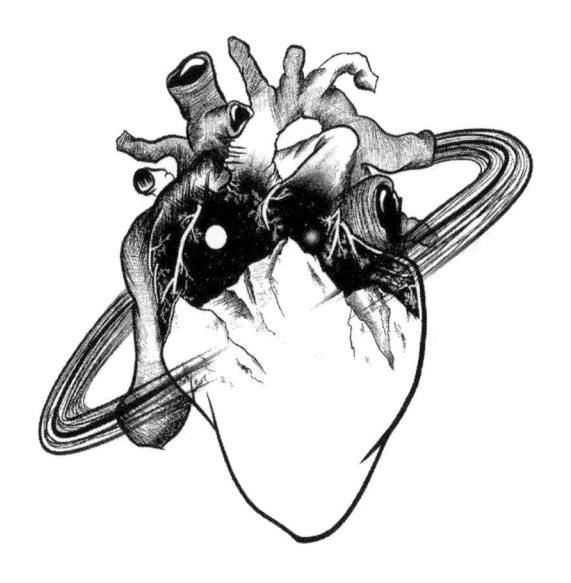

My reluctance to speak, don't mistake that for reluctance to love.

- I'll try.

My sister is quiet / I often find her in stillness / she is the most beautiful woman I have ever seen / you would *weep* if you held her in your eyes / my sister could break in your palms if you held on too tightly / I've tried / and how could I have ever not loved her as she loves me / the woman that helped raise me / the woman that showed me strength that came with honesty and pain and truth / I wish I had the strength that she has / as she holds her children / as she gives them a world so different to what she knew / my sister is strong and delicate / beyond the quiet / one and only

- Yau Chok.

How could she be so gentle / this is something I ask the universe / when this world is too cruel and wayward / has treated you with only harshness / brutality / yet you remain so loving / unyielding / little flower / you have grown so tall / you have grown with grace / incomparable / it is true what they say / the flowers that bloom last / bloom most beautifully

- Yau Lui.

I was not counting on your eyes to set within mine as the sun does the evening horizon in shades of lilac / lavender hue / I was not counting on your wide smile / wild laughter / to send vibrations down my spine / shivering / splitting the ice that stood between us / I was not counting on your fingertips / to awaken a fire in me / smouldering through the myriad of misconceptions I held about this feeling / I was not counting on you / to teach me that this world did indeed possess goodness / I have it now / this *gorgeous* thing / that had once been foreign / it had made a home inside of me

- That feeling.

Every crevice,

wound,

bruise,

and cut

on my soul.

We have arrived at a mutual understanding.

- Process.

A poem, can be a journey that
has always been with you, unnoticed
at times, until it becomes written. Then you can *mourn*.

- Seeker.

ABOUT THE AUTHOR

Born to a British mother and a Chinese father in Birmingham, England in 1994; Samantha Yau spent her early childhood in her father's native Hong Kong and later returned to Acocks Green, Birmingham. She graduated from Newman University with a degree in Psychology and has been writing poetically for the last nine years in recluse. During the pandemic of 2020, she felt encouraged to change and began sharing her poetry online. She is an educator in the West Midlands and has had poetry published with the Quillkeepers Press, Poets Against Poverty and the Folklore Prize. You can connect with her on Instagram (@smlyau) and at her website (smlyau.co.uk).

ABOUT THE ILLUSTRATOR

Born to Bangladeshi parents in 1994, Serina Yasmin spent her early years living with her grandparents in West Bromwich before moving to Acocks Green, Birmingham. With an early exposure to expression, she continued her passion, despite this being frowned upon by many, and went onto study Art & Design at the Birmingham School of Art. You can connect with Serina online (@ssycreates, Instagram), where she often posts about her journey, her art & designs.

Printed in Great Britain
by Amazon